# Across the Curriculum: SCIENCE for ages 6–7

A wide range of teachers' notes and photocopiable worksheets to address the needs of teachers and pupils in covering several aspects of the curriculum, while learning valuable concepts in science.

# Across the Curriculum: Science for ages 6–7
## Contents

Page

### Unit 1 – 'Health and Growth'

| | |
|---|---|
| 4 | Web page showing curriculum links for 'Health and Growth' |
| 5 | Teachers' notes for 'Health and Growth' |
| 6 | 'Health and Growth' Worksheet 1 – Literacy |
| 7 | 'Health and Growth' Worksheet 2 – Literacy |
| 8 | 'Health and Growth' Worksheet 3 – DT/Literacy |
| 9 | 'Health and Growth' Worksheet 4 – DT/Art/Literacy |
| 10 | 'Health and Growth' Worksheet 5 – PE/Literacy |
| 11 | 'Health and Growth' Worksheet 6 – Numeracy |
| 12 | 'Health and Growth' Worksheet 7 – Numeracy |
| 13 | 'Health and Growth' Worksheet 8 – History/Literacy |

### Unit 2 – 'Plants and Animals'

| | |
|---|---|
| 14 | Web page showing curriculum links for 'Plants and Animals' |
| 15 | Teachers' notes for 'Plants and Animals' |
| 16 | 'Plants and Animals' Worksheet 1 – Literacy |
| 17 | 'Plants and Animals' Worksheet 2 – Literacy |
| 18 | 'Plants and Animals' Worksheet 3 – Literacy/Numeracy |
| 19 | 'Plants and Animals' Worksheet 4 – Literacy/Numeracy |
| 20 | 'Plants and Animals' Worksheet 5 – Art |
| 21 | 'Plants and Animals' Worksheet 6 – Geography |
| 22 | 'Plants and Animals' Worksheet 7 – Geography |
| 23 | 'Plants and Animals' Worksheet 8 – Numeracy |

### Unit 3 – 'Variation'

| | |
|---|---|
| 24 | Web page showing curriculum links for 'Variation' |
| 25 | Teachers' notes for 'Variation' |
| 26 | 'Variation' Worksheet 1 – Literacy |
| 27 | 'Variation' Worksheet 2 – Literacy/Art/DT |
| 28 | 'Variation' Worksheet 3 – Literacy/DT |
| 29 | 'Variation' Worksheet 4 – Literacy |
| 30 | 'Variation' Worksheet 5 – Literacy |
| 31 | 'Variation' Worksheet 6 – Literacy/RE |
| 32 | 'Variation' Worksheet 7 – RE/Literacy/Numeracy |
| 33 | 'Variation' Worksheet 8 – Numeracy |

# Across the Curriculum Science for ages 6–7
## Contents

Page | **Unit 4 – 'Grouping and Changing Materials'**
--- | ---
34 | Web page showing curriculum links for 'Grouping and Changing Materials'
35 | Teachers' notes for 'Grouping and Changing Materials'
36 | 'Grouping and Changing Materials' Worksheet 1 – Literacy
37 | 'Grouping and Changing Materials' Worksheet 2 – Literacy
38 | 'Grouping and Changing Materials' Worksheet 3 – Literacy
39 | 'Grouping and Changing Materials' Worksheet 4 – Literacy
40 | 'Grouping and Changing Materials' Worksheet 5 – Literacy/History
41 | 'Grouping and Changing Materials' Worksheet 6 – Literacy/History
42 | 'Grouping and Changing Materials' Worksheet 7 – Numeracy
43 | 'Grouping and Changing Materials' Worksheet 8 – DT
44 | 'Grouping and Changing Materials' Worksheet 9 – Art
45 | 'Grouping and Changing Materials' Worksheet 10 – Music

**Unit 5 – 'Forces and Movement'**

Page | 
--- | ---
46 | Web page showing curriculum links for 'Forces and Movement'
47 | Teachers' notes for 'Forces and Movement'
48 | 'Forces and Movement' Worksheet 1 – Literacy
49 | 'Forces and Movement' Worksheet 2 – Literacy
50 | 'Forces and Movement' Worksheet 3 – Literacy
51 | 'Forces and Movement' Worksheet 4 – Numeracy
52 | 'Forces and Movement' Worksheet 5 – Numeracy
53 | 'Forces and Movement' Worksheet 6 – DT
54 | 'Forces and Movement' Worksheet 7 – DT

**Unit 6 – 'Using Electricity'**

Page | 
--- | ---
55 | Web page showing curriculum links for 'Using Electricity'
56 | Teachers' notes for 'Using Electricity'
57 | 'Using Electricity' Worksheet 1 – Literacy
58 | 'Using Electricity' Worksheet 2 – Literacy
59 | 'Using Electricity' Worksheet 3 – Literacy
60 | 'Using Electricity' Worksheet 4 – Literacy
61 | 'Using Electricity' Worksheet 5 – Numeracy
62 | 'Using Electricity' Worksheet 6 – History
63 | 'Using Electricity' Worksheet 7 – History
64 | Spare web page for teachers' own use

Across the Curriculum: Science for ages 6–7

# HEALTH AND GROWTH

Curriculum Links

We show possible curriculum links but we will not have thought of everything so you may like to add some of your own.

**Health and Growth**

### Literacy
Language of time: before, after, during, when – see PE.
Alphabetical order of vocabulary: Life processes – grow, growth, move, young, reproduce, feed, adult, baby, babies, child, children.
Health – diet, variety, germs, healthy, unhealthy, medicines, safety, exercise.
Tastes – salty, sweet, sour.
Practise spellings of food types: carbohydrates, proteins, fruit, vegetables, fats, meat, fish, eggs, cheese, rice, pasta.
Syllables.
Plurals.

### PE
Use of vocabulary to describe PE: before, during, after, when, hot, cold, thirsty, tired.
Exercise: body, arms, legs.
Exercise through dance and gymnastics: warm-ups, sequences of balances and movement;
How did you feel before PE? What did you do in PE? Which parts of the body were exercised? How did you feel after PE?

### ICT
Constructing a pictogram of favourite foods.

### Art
Self portrait.
Produce photographs using a digital camera.

### History
Florence Nightingale

### Numeracy
Block graphs of different types of food: survey of favourite foods.
'What is your favourite vegetable?' (give list)
'What is your favourite fruit?' (give list)

### DT
Food. Not related to any of the DT topics listed by QCA but referred to in the Science as 'DT food'. Plan a meal with balanced diet: Picture of plate: draw an appropriately balanced meal.

Andrew Brodie Publications © A & C Black Publishers Ltd.

# HEALTH AND GROWTH

**Across the Curriculum — Science for ages 6–7 — Teachers' Notes**

Worksheets 1 and 2 are used together. Not only do they include a large collection of technical scientific vocabulary but they also provide an opportunity for sorting words into alphabetical order in accordance with the Literacy Strategy. Children should notice that not every letter of the alphabet is represented, but that some letters have several words. They should be encouraged to observe that many words are related: health, healthy, unhealthy, etc.

Worksheet 3 provides further vocabulary that is particularly relevant to the topic. This sheet introduces Worksheet 4, where children are asked to draw a plate of food to illustrate a balanced diet. They are prompted to include at least two items from the lists of fruit and vegetables, then one item from each of the protein and carbohydrates lists, thus encouraging the idea that fruit and vegetables are important.

Worksheet 5 should be read very carefully before the children start a PE lesson. You may find it helpful to read the sheet through with the children during a literacy lesson so that they are not too desperate to go straight to PE, and may give more thought to what they will need to consider. Again, a variety of useful and relevant vocabulary is introduced.

Before children draw their own bar charts it is helpful to look at a pre-prepared chart, considering what it shows and what it means. Worksheet 6 provides a prepared bar chart on the subject of favourite fruits. After answering the questions on the sheet some children will also be able to answer the question, 'How many people took part in the survey?'

Worksheet 7 is a recording sheet for an investigation about favourite fruits amongst classmates. When the children have gathered the raw data, they need to enter it on the bar chart template provided. This should be marked with appropriate titles, including an overall title and titles for each axis.

Worksheet 8 is a literacy and history comprehension sheet about Florence Nightingale. Florence Nightingale was famous for improving hygiene conditions in medical treatment areas. Opportunity could be taken to remind children of the importance of personal hygiene for good health.

**1** Across the Curriculum: Science for ages 6–7 **HEALTH AND GROWTH**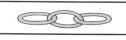

Literacy

Name:  Date:

## Useful words

Here are some words we may use when working on <u>Health and Growth</u>.

Write the words on the alphabet sheet. Write each word next to the correct letter of the alphabet.

<u>life processes</u>
grow   young   baby
reproduce   adult
child   growing   move
breathe   babies
feed   growth   children

<u>health</u>
health   diet
food   germs   safe
unhealthy   safety
medicines   healthy
exercise

<u>tastes</u>
salty   sweet   sour
bitter

<u>food types</u>
carbohydrates   fats
proteins   fruit
vegetables

<u>food</u>
meat   fish   eggs
cheese   rice
pasta   potatoes
cereals

<u>drinks</u>
water   milk

<u>time</u>
before   after
during   when

Andrew Brodie Publications © A & C Black Publishers Ltd.

| Across the Curriculum: Science for ages 6–7 | HEALTH AND GROWTH |  Literacy | 2 |

Name:                                          Date:

## Alphabet sheet

a b c d e f g h i j k l m n o p q r s t u v w x y z

(worksheet grid with empty boxes for students to write words beginning with each letter: a, b, c, d, e, f, g, h, m, p, r, s, u, v, w, y)

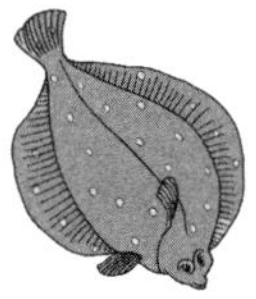

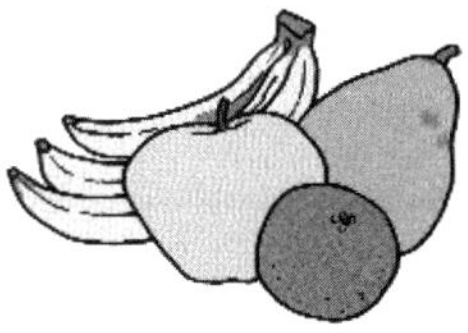

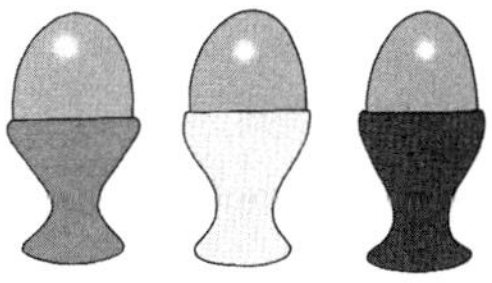

| **3** Across the Curriculum: Science for ages 6–7 | **HEALTH AND GROWTH** |  DT/Literacy |

Name:              Date:

### Getting a balanced meal

In a meal you need a balance of food types. Choose some food for a lunch plate.

You should have at least two items from the fruit and vegetables lists. You should have one item from the proteins list and one item from the carbohydrate list.

Practise spelling the words in each group.

<u>vegetables</u>                             <u>fruit</u>

carrots _____      apple _____

beans _____      orange _____

cabbage _____      banana _____

pepper _____      pineapple _____

onions _____      mango _____

cauliflower _____      passion fruit _____

okra _____      kiwi _____

aubergine _____      star fruit _____

<u>proteins</u>                             <u>carbohydrates</u>

meat _____      potatoes _____

fish _____      pasta _____

cheese _____      rice _____

eggs _____      bread _____

Andrew Brodie Publications © A & C Black Publishers Ltd.

Across the Curriculum: Science for ages 6–7

# HEALTH AND GROWTH

DT/Art/Literacy

**4**

Name:  Date:

## Drawing lunch

Draw and label a plate of food for lunch.

Don't forget, you need a balanced diet.

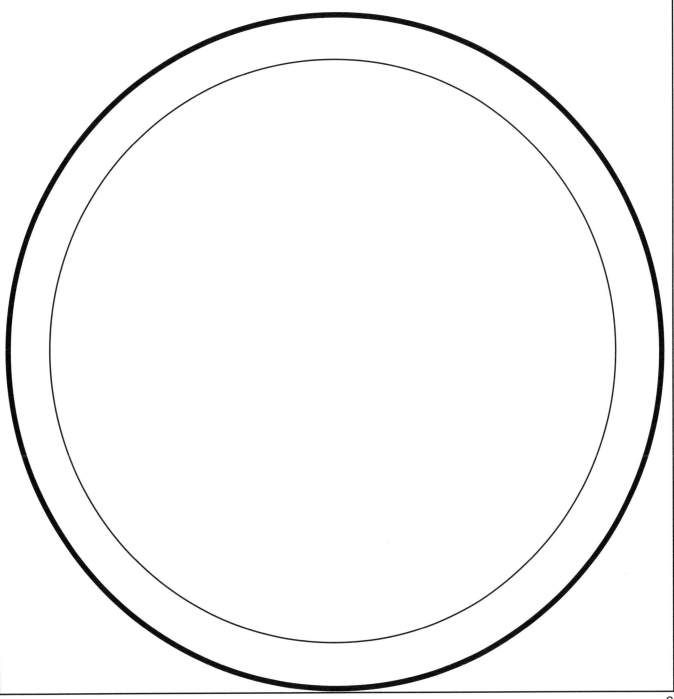

# HEALTH AND GROWTH

*Across the Curriculum: Science for ages 6–7* — PE/Literacy

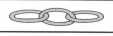

Name:  Date:

## A PE lesson

**WORD BANK**

hot   cold   tired   energetic   lazy   arms
legs   ankles   wrists   knees   exercise   neck
shoulders   head   fingers   hands
gymnastics   dance   warm-up   cool-down
out of breath   exhausted

How did you feel <u>before</u> PE today?
_____
_____

What did you do in PE today?
_____
_____

How did you feel <u>during</u> PE?
_____
_____

Which parts of your body did you exercise?
_____
_____

How did you feel <u>after</u> PE?
_____
_____

What was the best part of the PE lesson?
_____

## Our favourite fruit

Some children were asked the question, 'What is your favourite fruit?' Here is a bar chart to show the answers.

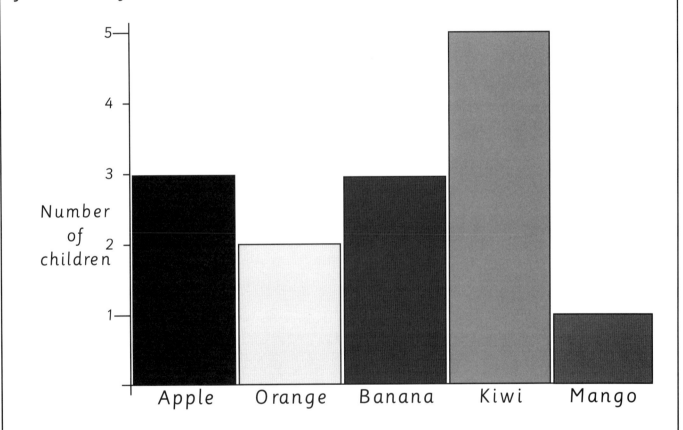

Which was the most popular fruit?

How many people liked it best?

Which was the least popular fruit?

How many people liked it best?

How many people liked apples best?

How many people liked oranges best?

How many people liked bananas best?

## Across the Curriculum: Science for ages 6–7

**HEALTH AND GROWTH** — Numeracy

Name:                        Date:

## Fruit survey

Here are the names of some fruits.

| apple | orange | banana | kiwi | mango |
|---|---|---|---|---|
|  |  |  |  |  |

Ask twelve children to choose their favourite of these fruits.
They should put one tick in the box for the fruit they like best.

Count the ticks in each box.
Draw a bar chart to show the results.

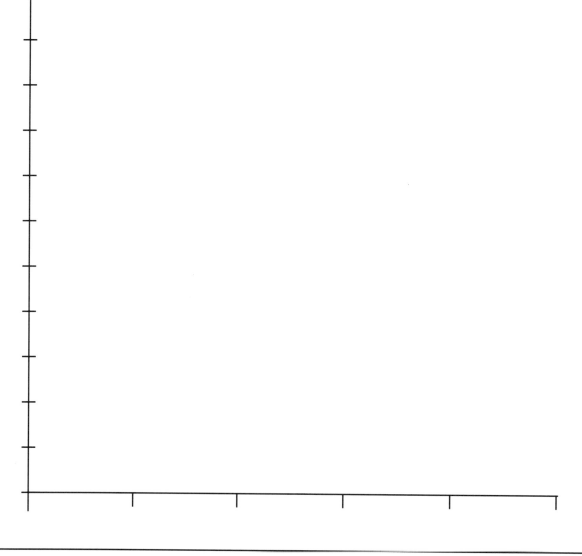

Across the Curriculum: Science for ages 6–7 | **HEALTH AND GROWTH** | History/Literacy | **8**

Name:                                Date:

### Florence Nightingale

Florence Nightingale was a very famous nurse. She was born on 12th May 1820. In Victorian times, hospitals were very different from today. Florence Nightingale knew how important it was to keep everything clean.

In 1854 she went to nurse wounded soldiers in the Crimean War. The soldiers called her 'the lady with the lamp'.

After the war she wrote books about nursing and started a training school for nurses. Florence Nightingale died in 1910. She was ninety years old.

- When was Florence Nightingale born?

_____

- What did she think was very important?

_____

- Who did she look after in the Crimean War?

_____

- What was their description for her?

_____

- When did Florence Nightingale die?

_____

Andrew Brodie Publications © A & C Black Publishers Ltd.

Across the Curriculum
Science for ages 6–7

# PLANTS AND ANIMALS

Curriculum Links

We show possible curriculum links but we will not have thought of everything so you may like to add some of your own.

**Plants and animals in the local environment.**

### Literacy
Use of context for reading. Vocabulary of life processes: produce new plants, produce young, reproduce. Names for animals: worm, slug, snail, fly, wasp, bee. Names for plants: grass, daisy, dandelions, oak tree, buttercup. Words in other context: short, fruit, earth, table. Location: next to, near. Instruction sheet: how to plant bean seeds in a jam jar with blotting-paper. Writing in sentences using capital letters and full stops.

### RE
Treating animals and plants carefully.

### ICT
Use a digital camera to make a series of photographs of a broad bean growing.

### Art
Plant a broad bean in the side of a jam jar – observational drawings as the bean grows.

### Geography
Understanding of place. Walk around school to discover where animals are found: snail, worm, woodlouse, etc. (See also Year 1.)

### Numeracy
Tables about plant growth. Table of plants/animals found. Measuring water using measuring cylinder, to put with bean in jam jar. Using a ruler to the nearest cm: measuring growth of the broad bean.

| Across the Curriculum Science for ages 6–7 | **PLANTS AND ANIMALS** | Teachers' Notes |

Worksheets 1 and 2 are used together. Not only do they include a large collection of technical scientific vocabulary but they also provide an opportunity for sorting words into alphabetical order in accordance with the Literacy Strategy. Children should notice that not every letter of the alphabet is represented, but that some letters of the alphabet have several words.

Worksheets 3 and 4 provide step by step instructions for children to follow, in order to 'plant' beans to observe their growth. This clearly involves literacy work in following relevant written instructions, but also includes numeracy work in making use of rulers and tape measures to measure blotting paper.

Worksheet 5 is used as a follow-up to planting the bean as instructed on Worksheets 3 and 4. Our two characters provide clues for the children to remind them to observe very carefully.

Worksheet 6 encourages children to observe their school grounds, gaining awareness of place – an important aspect of geography. We have provided illustrations of plants that are likely to be found in most school grounds, but children may find others that can be listed instead.

Worksheet 7 is similar to Worksheet 6 but concerns animals instead of plants. Again, children gain awareness of place. They should be encouraged to consider why particular animals are found in particular places, thus beginning to develop an understanding of habitat. Habitats will be considered further in Year 4.

Worksheet 8 provides practice of measurement using standard units.

Andrew Brodie Publications © A & C Black Publishers Ltd.

# PLANTS AND ANIMALS

**1** Across the Curriculum: Science for ages 6–7

Literacy

Name:    Date:

## Useful words

*Here are some words we may use when working on Plants and Animals.*

*Write the words on the alphabet sheet. Write each word next to the correct letter of the alphabet.*

### life processes
produce   new   plants
reproduce   young

### birds
sparrow   blackbird
starling   robin
chaffinch

### animals
worm   slug   snail   fly
wasp   bee   spider
woodlouse   centipede
millipede

### plants
grass   daisy
dandelion   buttercup

### trees
oak   apple   sycamore
birch   beech   ash
maple   pine

### places
under   next   near
over   above
beneath

*Birds are animals.*

*Trees are plants.*

Andrew Brodie Publications © A & C Black Publishers Ltd.

| Across the Curriculum: Science for ages 6–7 | **PLANTS AND ANIMALS** | Literacy | 2 |

Name:     Date:

## Alphabet sheet

a b c d e f g h i j k l m n o p q r s t u v w x y z

a
b
c
d
f
g 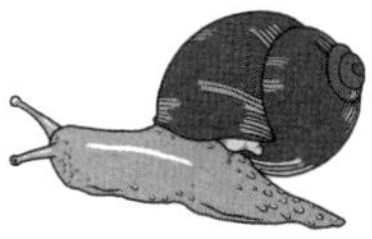 
m
n
o
p
r
s
u
w
y

Andrew Brodie Publications © A & C Black Publishers Ltd.

**3** Across the Curriculum: Science for ages 6–7

**PLANTS AND ANIMALS**

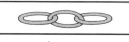

Literacy/Numeracy

Name:  Date:

# Planting some beans

You will need:

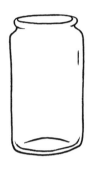
jam jar

blotting paper

two beans

water

1  Measure the height of the jam jar.

What is its height? ☐

Subtract 3cm ⟶ ☐

This is the height of blotting paper you need.

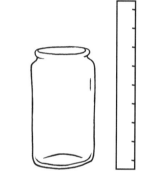

2  Measure around the jam jar.

What is its circumference?

Add 2cm ⟶

This is the length of blotting paper you need.

3  Cut out the blotting paper you need.

Andrew Brodie Publications © A & C Black Publishers Ltd.

## Planting some beans

4 Put the blotting paper in the jam jar, so that it curls around the inner surface of the glass.

5 Push two beans between the blotting paper and the glass.

6 Pour some water in the bottom of the jar.

7 Wait for the beans to grow.

8 Observe the beans carefully.

# PLANTS AND ANIMALS

**5** — Across the Curriculum: Science for ages 6–7 — Art

Name:        Date:

## Growing a bean

*Look at the bean in the jar. Look very carefully.*

*Can you see any roots? Can you see any shoots?*

Draw the bean every day.

| | | |
|---|---|---|
| | | |
| _____ | _____ | _____ |
| | | |
| _____ | _____ | _____ |

Across the Curriculum: Science for ages 6–7 | **PLANTS AND ANIMALS** | Geography | **6**

Name:  Date:

## Plant hunt

You are going on a plant hunt. Be careful not to damage the plants.

daisy    grass    dandelion    buttercup

Fill in the table. Here are some useful words:

**damp    dry    wet    shady    sunny**

| Name of plant | Place where found | Description of place |
|---|---|---|
|  |  |  |
|  |  |  |
|  |  |  |
|  |  |  |

Andrew Brodie Publications © A & C Black Publishers Ltd.

**7** Across the Curriculum: Science for ages 6–7

# PLANTS AND ANIMALS

Geography

Name:          Date:

## Animal hunt

You are going on an animal hunt. Be careful not to hurt the animals.

*Write the names of animals you find on the chart.*

*Write down where you find each animal. What is each place like?*

Here are some useful words:

**damp   wet   dry   moist   dark   light   cold   warm
worm   slug   snail   fly   wasp   bee   spider
woodlouse   centipede   millipede**

| Name of animal | Place where found | Description of place |
|---|---|---|
|  |  |  |
|  |  |  |
|  |  |  |
|  |  |  |
|  |  |  |
|  |  |  |
|  |  |  |
|  |  |  |
|  |  |  |
|  |  |  |

Andrew Brodie Publications © A & C Black Publishers Ltd.

Across the Curriculum: Science for ages 6–7

# PLANTS AND ANIMALS

Numeracy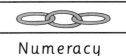

**8**

Name:                                    Date:

## How long is a worm?

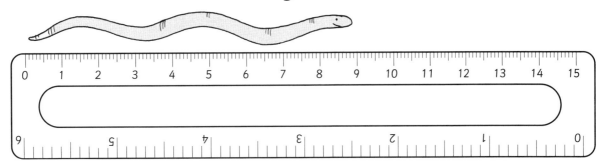

This worm is approximately nine centimetres long.

We can write nine centimetres like this : 9cm.

Measure each worm and write a sentence about its length.

●

_____

_____

●

_____

_____

●

_____

_____

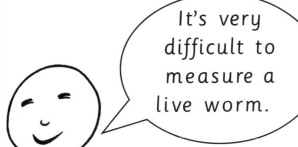

It's very difficult to measure a live worm.

But you could use your ruler to measure the heights of some plants.

Andrew Brodie Publications © A & C Black Publishers Ltd.

| Across the Curriculum Science for ages 6–7 | **VARIATION** |  Curriculum Links |

We show possible curriculum links but we will not have thought of everything so you may like to add some of your own.

## Variation

**Literacy**
Vocabulary: words naming features of animals and plants, e.g. feathers, fur, shell, branch, claws, paws, wings, scales, two-legged, four-legged, spikes, snout, ears, sting, leaf, root, tree, shoot.
Comparatives: long, longer, longest.
Generalisations: 'we all', 'must have'.
Pictures of animals/plants – group into animals or plants. Reasons why some things are animals and are not plants.
Descriptions – why animals are like each other.

**RE**
Treating animals with care.
Noah's Ark: measured in cubits; variation in cubit sizes.

**Art**
Make drawings of plants: label stem, leaf, root, flowers, branch.
Drawing pairs of animals for Noah's Ark.

**Geography**
Observations of local plants.
Seaside: plants, creatures, variety.

**Numeracy**
Measurements of length using standard units (measuring leaves).
Measure hand-span in centimetres.
– recognise differences;
– tally chart and block graph to show findings;
– number of children with particular size of hand-span;
– asking questions about what the block graph shows;
– measuring cubit;
– measuring around head.
(Activity could be in groups of six with classroom assistant.)

Andrew Brodie Publications © A & C Black Publishers Ltd.

**Across the Curriculum
Science for ages 6–7**

**VARIATION**

**Teachers' Notes**

Worksheet 1 is a vocabulary sheet, containing words related to the topic of variation.

Worksheets 2 and 3 are used together. They incorporate relevant spelling practice as well as providing opportunities to discuss similarities and differences between plants and animals. The children should be asked to explain why some organisms are classified as plants and some are classified as animals. For example, they could be asked whether an oak tree is a plant or an animal. Hopefully they will reply that it is a plant and they can then be asked the more difficult questions of why it is a plant and why it is not an animal. These type of questions help to develop children' logical thinking and their abilities in speaking and listening. This discussion should help the children when they complete Worksheets 4 and 5.

Worksheet 6 retells, in very simple terms, the story of Noah and the ark. This could be followed by art work, showing the huge variety of animals that would have been present on the ark – an ideal large scale wall display. We have deliberately included the non-standard measurements of cubits. A cubit was an ancient measurement of length, based on the elbow to the tip of the fingers. It therefore provides great opportunities for discussion of variation between humans; this could be centred on Worksheet 7.

Worksheet 8 provides practice of measurement using standard units and should promote discussion regarding variation between individuals.

# 1 Across the Curriculum: Science for ages 6–7

## VARIATION

Literacy

Name:  Date:

## Finding words about plants and animals

### Clues across

2. Animals hear with these: _ _ _ _ .
5. A large plant with leaves: _ _ _ _ _ .
6. Cats are four- _ _ _ _ _ _ , birds are two- _ _ _ _ _ _ _ .
9. Many animals are covered in _ _ _ .
11. Fish have _ _ _ _ _ _ on their body.
12. Hedgehogs have _ _ _ _ _ _ _ .
14. An animal's nose is sometimes called a _ _ _ _ _ _ .

### Clues down

1. Birds' bodies are covered with _ _ _ _ _ _ _ _ _ .
3. A snail has a _ _ _ _ _ _ .
4. A plant's _ _ _ _ carries water from the roots to the leaves.
7. A tree has _ _ _ _ _ _ _ _ _ joined to its trunk.
8. Most trees have green _ _ _ _ _ _ _ .
9. Animals and birds have _ _ _ _ at the bottom of their legs.
10. Birds use their _ _ _ _ _ to fly.
11. New growth on a plant is sometimes called a _ _ _ _ _ _ .
13. Wasps and bees can _ _ _ _ _ _ .

26  Andrew Brodie Publications © A & C Black Publishers Ltd.

Across the Curriculum: Science for ages 6–7

**VARIATION**

Literacy/Art/DT

2

Name:                               Date:

## Plant or animal?

Copy the words. Colour the pictures.
Cut the pictures out.
Stick them in the correct part of worksheet 3.

 oak tree

 robin

 mouse

 daisy

 spider

grass

 buttercup

 cat

Andrew Brodie Publications © A & C Black Publishers Ltd.

# 3 — Across the Curriculum: Science for ages 6–7

## VARIATION

Literacy/DT

Name:  
Date:

## Plant or animal?

| Plants | Animals |
|--------|---------|
|        |         |
|        |         |
|        |         |
|        |         |

Across the Curriculum: Science for ages 6–7 | **VARIATION** | Literacy | **4**

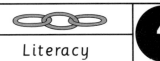

Name:            Date:

## The same or different?

Here is a plant.

Here is an animal.

Here are some words.

**WORD BANK**
alive    live    living
breathe    walk
move    grow
still    sleep    legs
stem    leaves
roots    flowers

In what ways are plants like animals?

_____
_____
_____
_____

In what ways are plants different to animals?

_____
_____
_____
_____

Andrew Brodie Publications © A & C Black Publishers Ltd.

# VARIATION

**Literacy**

Across the Curriculum: Science for ages 6–7 — 5

Name: _____ Date: _____

## The same or different?

Here is a human.

Here is a bird.

Here are some words.

**WORD BANK**

live   alive   living
breathe   move
wings   feathers
eyes   beak   legs
feet   mouth
nose   arms
hands   fly

In what ways are people like birds?

_____
_____
_____
_____
_____

In what ways are people different to birds?

_____
_____
_____
_____
_____

# Noah's Ark

The story of Noah's Ark tells us that God decided to flood the world because most people were bad. God chose to save eight people: Noah and his wife, their three sons and their wives.

God told Noah to build a big boat called an ark. The ark had to be three hundred cubits long, fifty cubits wide and thirty cubits high.

God said that Noah had to find a pair of every type of animal. Noah had to take all these animals with him in the ark.

It rained and rained and rained. The world became flooded. Noah's ark floated on the water.

The sun came out and at last the land dried up. Noah let all the animals out of the ark.

## Cubits

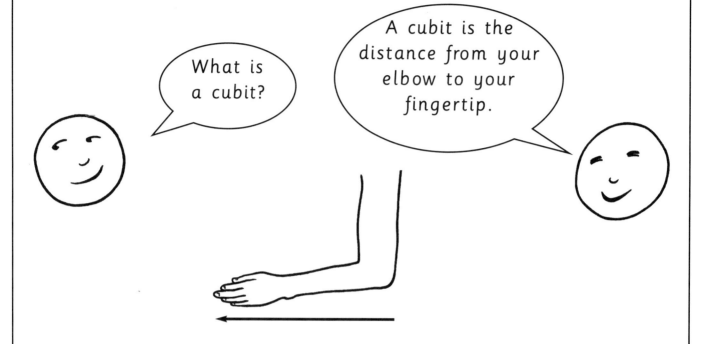

- Work with a partner.
- Measure the length of your cubit in centimetres.

    My cubit is _____ centimetres long.

- Measure your partner's cubit.

    My partner's cubit is _____ centimetres long.

- Measure an adult's cubit.

    The adult's cubit is _____ centimetres long.

- Who has the longest cubit? _____

- Who has the shortest cubit? _____

- Why is the cubit not a very good unit to measure things with?
  _____
  _____

Across the Curriculum: Science for ages 6–7

**VARIATION**

Numeracy

8

Name:  Date:

## Measuring parts of the body

Work with a partner. Use a tape measure.

Measure the parts of the body shown on this page. Write the two sets of results on the chart.

handspan

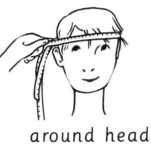
around head

around wrist

length of foot

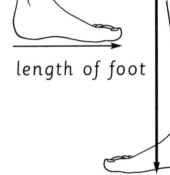
knee to floor

around knee

| Measurements | Name | Name |
|---|---|---|
| hand span | | |
| around head | | |
| length of foot | | |
| knee height | | |
| around knee | | |
| around wrist | | |

Andrew Brodie Publications © A & C Black Publishers Ltd.

# Grouping and Changing Materials

**Across the Curriculum Science for ages 6–7**

**Curriculum Links**

We show possible curriculum links but we will not have thought of everything so you may like to add some of your own.

**Literacy**
Vocabulary – alphabetical order.

**Music**
Materials used in instruments and the effect the materials have on the sound produced.

**Art**
Drawing a car and labelling it according to different materials used for different purposes. Weaving with paper.

**History**
The Great Fire of London. Relevance of the materials used for construction of buildings, before and after the fire.

**Grouping and Changing Materials**

**DT**
Mechanisms – what vehicles are made from. Weaving with paper.

**Geography**
Selection of items from other countries to sort according to the materials from which they are made.

**Numeracy**
Data collection: examining familiar items and sorting them according to materials.

| Across the Curriculum | GROUPING AND | Teachers' |
| Science for ages 6–7 | CHANGING MATERIALS | Notes |

Worksheet 1 is concerned with the correct vocabulary for changes in form of materials when subjected to temperature changes. Most of the sentences are connected with the properties of water, but we have included one sentence regarding change in form of butter. You may wish to extend the activity by asking children to think of other materials that change in form when heated or cooled.

Worksheet 2 is a vocabulary sheet, based on opposites and comparative adjectives.

Worksheet 3 also features vocabulary relevant to the topic, together with an activity for sorting words related to materials.

Worksheet 4 provides a relevant activity for alphabetical order.

Worksheets 5 and 6 are centred around the story of the Great Fire of London. They provide excellent revision of work if this topic has already been covered for history, while helping children to become more aware of the relevance of using appropriate materials.

For Worksheet 7, you will need to provide a variety of items for the children to examine – ideally as many as twenty different items.

Worksheet 8 features an illustration of a car for children to label according to the materials used in its construction. To complete this work groups of children should ideally have the opportunity to 'examine' a real vehicle in a safe environment. This activity can be extended by adding extra labels to the worksheet.

Worksheet 9: Weaving – resources needed: worksheet photocopied onto thin card, selection of paper, card, foil, polythene, etc., cut into strips approximately 20cm x 1cm, stapler or tape to hold finished weaving in place. This activity also helps with assessment if children complete the top and bottom portions.
Note: Children may need help cutting along marked lines.

Worksheet 10 shows a selection of musical instruments. For children to complete this sheet, ideally they will need an appropriate selection of instruments to work with. Before starting to complete the chart it is ideal to discuss how each instrument is made and played and to ask children for their own ideas about the sounds made. Children should not be restricted to the suggested words for use in the final column.

Andrew Brodie Publications © A & C Black Publishers Ltd.

| 1 | Across the Curriculum: Science for ages 6–7 | GROUPING AND CHANGING MATERIALS | Literacy |

Name:    Date:

## Changes

 You need to know how materials 'change' to do this work.

Choose the correct word to put in the sentence.
The first one has been done for you.

- When water <u>freezes</u> it turns to ice.

    pours    boils    freezes

- When water _____ it turns into steam.

    pours    boils    freezes

- Sugar _____ in water.

    dissolves    steams    freezes

- Butter _____ when it is warmed.

    freezes    cools    melts

- To melt ice put it somewhere _____ .

    warm    fridge    drink

- Put water in the freezer to turn it into ____ .

    water    steam    ice

| Across the Curriculum: Science for ages 6–7 | **GROUPING AND CHANGING MATERIALS** | Literacy | **2** |

| Name: | Date: |

## Opposites

- Look in the box to find the opposite of each of the words below.
- Write each opposite beside the word.

**WORD BANK**
soft   cool   stretch
hot   freeze

- hard ⟶ _____
- thaw ⟶ _____
- squeeze ⟶ _____
- heat ⟶ _____
- cold ⟶ _____

### Comparative adjectives

Complete the table below. The first line has been done for you.

| | | |
|---|---|---|
| hot | hotter | hottest |
| cold | | |
| | warmer | |
| | | coolest |
| hard | | |
| | | softest |

Andrew Brodie Publications © A & C Black Publishers Ltd.

# GROUPING AND CHANGING MATERIALS

**3** Across the Curriculum: Science for ages 6–7

Literacy

Name:   Date:

## Wordsearch

Find the words from the box in the wordsearch.

**WORD BANK**

egg   metal   flour
pebbles   sugar
sand   rubber
butter   stones
glass   shells
milk

The words may be written horizontally, →
vertically ↓ or diagonally. ↘
Shade the words lightly as you find them.

| a | l | c | t | b | e | g | g | d | f | n | e | b |
|---|---|---|---|---|---|---|---|---|---|---|---|---|
| r | s | n | d | e | l | f | l | o | u | r | l | u |
| q | u | b | e | t | e | t | a | o | g | c | t | t |
| p | t | b | b | i | r | h | s | z | e | u | r | t |
| p | e | b | b | l | e | s | s | a | n | d | s | e |
| a | p | n | t | e | t | t | h | e | l | i | z | r |
| q | w | e | q | s | r | o | m | e | t | a | l | k |
| c | h | j | s | t | h | n | t | l | e | t | s | v |
| t | g | i | p | p | n | e | m | i | l | k | u | x |
| m | q | e | x | u | i | s | l | o | l | b | g | r |
| d | y | v | b | r | o | r | r | l | n | x | a | t |
| l | u | k | n | w | s | b | j | x | s | f | r | t |

Now sort the words into the correct places below.

Find these on the beach.

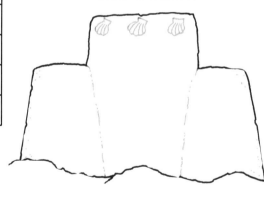

Use these to make a cake.

These may help make a car.

38   Andrew Brodie Publications © A & C Black Publishers Ltd.

| Across the Curriculum: Science for ages 6–7 | GROUPING AND CHANGING MATERIALS | Literacy  | 4 |

Name: _____  Date: _____

## Alphabetical order

- The words on this page are the names of 'materials' and the ways that they work.

- Arrange them in alphabetical order.

- Here is the alphabet to help you.

a b c d e f g h i j k l m n o p q r s t u v w x y z

**WORD BANK**

wood   clay   metal   bend

squash   hard   twist

glass   plastic   leather

natural   freeze

1. _____ 2. _____ 3. _____

4. _____ 5. _____ 6. _____

7. _____ 8. _____ 9. _____

10. _____ 11. _____ 12. _____

- Use your own words to write a meaning for each of the three words below.

natural _____
_____

glass _____
_____

wood _____
_____

Andrew Brodie Publications © A & C Black Publishers Ltd.

Across the Curriculum: Science for ages 6–7

**GROUPING AND CHANGING MATERIALS**

 Literacy/History

Name:                                Date:

## The Great Fire of London

The Great Fire of London began on 2nd September 1666. It started at a bakery in a street called Pudding Lane.

Most of the houses in London at that time were made of wood so the fire spread very quickly.

Many people escaped the fire by going along the River Thames in boats.

The fire burned for five days. More than thirteen thousand buildings burned down.

After the fire people knew that building new houses of wood was not a good idea so their new homes were made of bricks.

Now answer the questions on the next page.

Andrew Brodie Publications © A & C Black Publishers Ltd.

Across the Curriculum: Science for ages 6–7

**GROUPING AND CHANGING MATERIALS**

Literacy/History

Name:                    Date:

# The Great Fire of London

Answer the questions carefully!

Ring the correct answer.

- In which month was the Fire of London?

  January        July        November        September

- In which year was the Fire of London?

  1955        1956        1666        1777

- What was the name of the street where it began?

  Pie Lane        Pudding Road        Pudding Lane        Cake Lane

- For how many days did the fire burn?

  5 days        5 weeks        13 days        5000 days

Now answer these questions.

- Why was it a good idea to escape the fire by boat?

  _____

  _____

- Why was it not a good idea to build all the houses from wood?

  _____

  _____

- Why was brick used to build new homes?

  _____

Andrew Brodie Publications © A & C Black Publishers Ltd.

**7** Across the Curriculum: Science for ages 6–7

## GROUPING AND CHANGING MATERIALS

Numeracy

Name:                                    Date:

## What's it made of?

- There are lots of items on the table.

- Decide whether each item is made from natural materials, man-made materials or both.

- Enter your results on the chart below by shading the blocks. Use a different colour for each column.

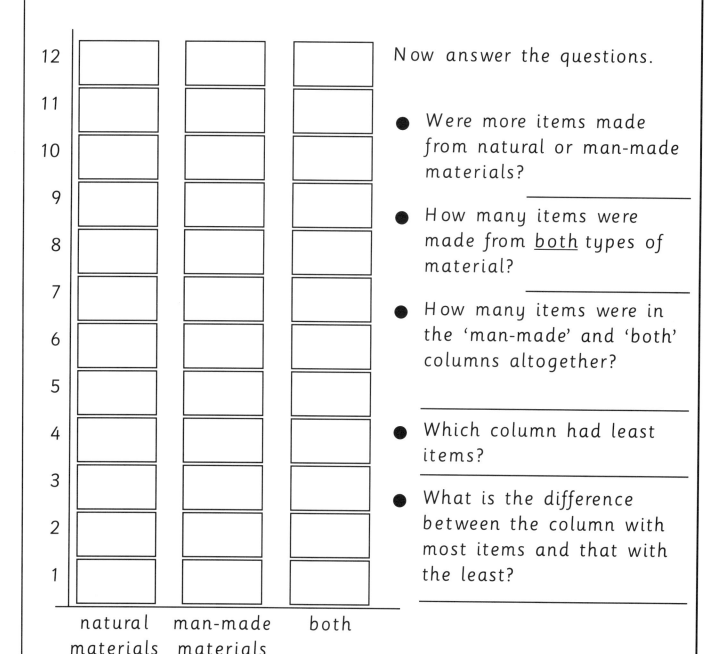

Now answer the questions.

- Were more items made from natural or man-made materials?
  _____

- How many items were made from <u>both</u> types of material?
  _____

- How many items were in the 'man-made' and 'both' columns altogether?
  _____

- Which column had least items?
  _____

- What is the difference between the column with most items and that with the least?

Andrew Brodie Publications © A & C Black Publishers Ltd.

Across the Curriculum: Science for ages 6–7

## GROUPING AND CHANGING MATERIALS

DT

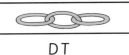

8

Name:                           Date:

## What are cars made of?

- You are going to look at a car. Please be very careful.
- On the plan below label the materials found on different parts of the car.

One has been completed for you.

| WORD BANK |
|---|
| metal    wood    leather |
| glass    rubber    plastic |
| cloth    other |

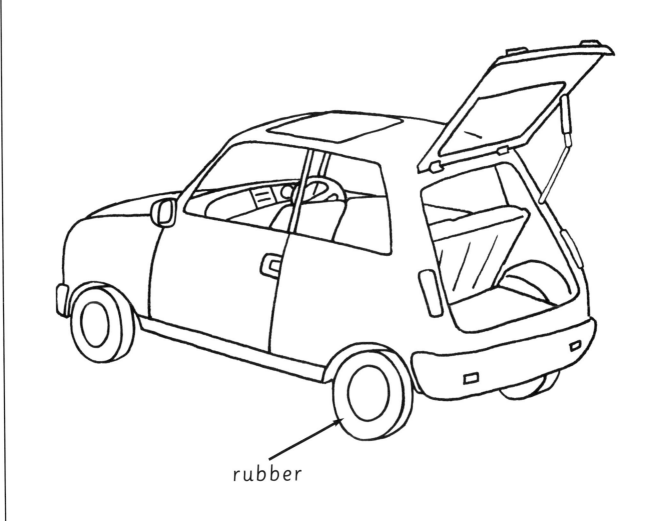

rubber

Andrew Brodie Publications © A & C Black Publishers Ltd.

**Across the Curriculum: Science for ages 6–7**

**GROUPING AND CHANGING MATERIALS**

Art

Name: _____   Date: _____

## Weaving

- Materials I have chosen for my weaving: _____
  _____

- Why I chose them: _____
  _____

- Am I pleased with my weaving? _____

- This is because: _____

*Cut along each of these lines.*

Andrew Brodie Publications © A & C Black Publishers Ltd.

Across the Curriculum: Science for ages 6–7

**GROUPING AND CHANGING MATERIALS**

Music

10

Name:

Date:

## Musical instruments

- Look at the instruments you have been given.
- Next to the pictures below write the name of the instrument, the materials from which it is made and a word to describe the sort of sound it makes.
- The word box may help you.

**WORD BANK**

metal   wood   plastic

triangle   drum   recorder

tambourine   xylophone

ting   tinkle   bang   whistle

| | Name | Material | Sound it makes |
|---|---|---|---|
| | | | |
| | | | |
| | | | |
| | | | |
| | | | |

Andrew Brodie Publications © A & C Black Publishers Ltd.

Across the Curriculum
Science for ages 6–7

# FORCES AND MOVEMENT

Curriculum Links

We show possible curriculum links but we will not have thought of everything so you may like to add some of your own.

**Literacy**
Word bank – alphabetical order of vocabulary related to forces and movement. Vowels – further vocabulary practice.

**PE**
Forces of pushing and pulling in all aspects of PE (kicking ball, etc.). Methods of moving our own bodies: bending and stretching.

**ICT**
Art package to create pictures to illustrate words from the word bank.

**Forces and Movement**

**History**
How people travelled in the past.

**DT**
Wheeled vehicle making. 'Yacht' making. Investigations and challenges.

**Geography**
How to get to an island. Links with DT boat making.

**Numeracy**
Measuring using standard measurements. Comparing results of an investigation.

| Across the Curriculum Science for ages 6–7 | **FORCES AND MOVEMENT** | Teachers' Notes |

Worksheet 1 provides a word bank that is ideal for enlarging and displaying in the classroom, but can also be used as a spelling sheet. An ICT art package could be used to create pictures inspired by one or more of the words from the word bank. This will need group discussion and sharing of ideas first. (For example, stop, go – illustrated by a car at traffic lights.)

Worksheet 2 can be used in conjunction with Worksheet 1. It contains many of the same words, but this time with their vowels omitted.

Worksheet 3 requires children to link movement words to illustrations. This activity could be extended by asking children to find more movement words and to illustrate them themselves.

Worksheet 4. – The science 'forces and movement' topic allows ample opportunity for beginning to use standard measures, and for basic graph work. We have provided lines to be measured that represent distances travelled by micro cars. An ideal extension activity would be for a small group of children to experiment with toy cars themselves, measuring distances travelled. The idea of fair testing could be discussed and children could be encouraged to think of ways to test fairly.

Worksheet 5 provides a follow up to Worksheet 4, asking children to interpret the data shown.

Worksheet 6 consists of a set of instructions for children to build a wind-powered boat. This is an activity for pairs or threes.
Resources: range of suitable 'boat building' materials: small margarine tubs, small foil containers, small pieces of light wood (for hull), straws (for masts), paper, thin card, plastic, polythene (for sails). Children may also request other items. The small items used for the hulls should prevent over-sized boats being built.
The activity should culminate in children helping to suggest a test. They may suggest blowing: this can be done but children should be encouraged to understand that this is not a fair test as some children can blow harder than others. One way of creating a fair test is by using a simple safe battery-operated hand fan. Emphasise the importance of the distance the fan is from the boats; namely the same each time.
To determine the results, you could:
 – time the boats to see how long each takes to travel the length of the container (these results can be used in a simple graph); or
 – race them one against another until the fastest is found; or
 – measure how far each boat travels in a set time (this is also good for simple graph work).
Note: In the course of the investigation it is important that the children recognise that the air/wind is propelling the boat by 'pushing'.

Worksheet 7. Build a vehicle – an activity best suited to pairs or threes.
Resources needed – a range of construction toys (with wheels).
Encourage children to think about the size of their vehicle, the best way of constructing it, and how well it carries its roll of tape.
When all the pairs/groups have produced a vehicle help them to think of ways to test it. First ensure they have a criteria against which to judge their vehicles. For example: fastest, furthest, which carries 1 roll of tape well (without rattling about or falling off).

| | **1** | Across the Curriculum: Science for ages 6–7 | **FORCES AND MOVEMENT** | Literacy |

Name:                              Date:

## Word bank

- These are useful words to read and spell when doing work on forces and movement.
- They have been arranged in alphabetical order.

| bend | furthest | right |
| --- | --- | --- |
| change | go | slow |
| direction | left | slower |
| distance | near | squeeze |
| far | press | start |
| fast | pull | stretch |
| force | push | turn |
| further | quickly | twist |

Andrew Brodie Publications © A & C Black Publishers Ltd.

| Across the Curriculum: Science for ages 6–7 | **FORCES AND MOVEMENT** | Literacy | 2 |

Name: | Date:

## Find the vowels

- Here are some of the words from the word bank.
- The vowels are missing.
- Put the vowels back into the words.

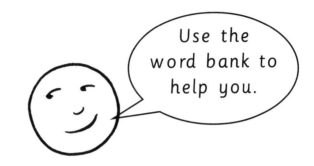

Use the word bank to help you.

### <u>a</u>  <u>e</u>  <u>i</u>  <u>o</u>  <u>u</u>

| b _ nd | d _ st _ nce | st _ p |
| ch _ ng _ | g _ | str _ tch |
| l _ ft | r _ ght | sq _ _ _ z _ |
| f _ r | n _ _ r | f _ rc _ |
| f _ st | sl _ w | pr _ ss |
| p _ sh | p _ ll | d _ r _ ct _ _ n |
| tw _ st | t _ rn | st _ rt |

Andrew Brodie Publications © A & C Black Publishers Ltd.

# FORCES AND MOVEMENT

*Across the Curriculum: Science for ages 6–7*

Literacy

Name:                               Date:

## Movement words

• Use the words from the box to caption the pictures.

**WORD BANK**

turn   push   twist
stretch   pull   bend

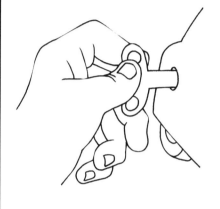

_____   _____   _____

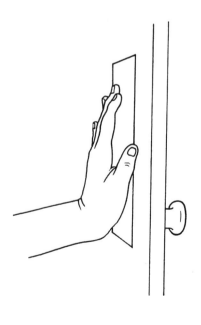
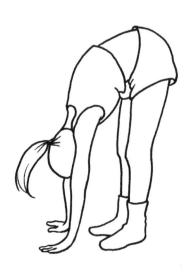

_____   _____   _____

Now you may colour the pictures.

# Across the Curriculum: Science for ages 6–7

## FORCES AND MOVEMENT

Numeracy

**4**

Name:

Date:

## Micro cars

A group of children carried out a very small investigation. They pushed their micro cars to see how far they moved. This shows where the cars started and stopped.

*When you have finished, see if you can answer the questions on worksheet 5.*

Measure each line to find out how far each car travelled. Write the measurement in centimetres on each line.

Ali — cm
Sara — cm
Joe — cm
Amy — cm
Matt — cm
Josh — cm
Leah — cm
Bob — cm

Andrew Brodie Publications © A & C Black Publishers Ltd.

**5** | Across the Curriculum: Science for ages 6–7 | **FORCES AND MOVEMENT** |  Numeracy

Name:           Date:

## Micro cars

Use the information on the previous page to answer the questions below.

- How many children did the investigation with their micro cars? _____

- Whose car travelled the furthest? _____
  How far did it travel? _____

- Name the three children whose cars went the same distance.
  _____    _____    _____

- How far did their cars travel? _____

- Name the two children whose cars moved just 6 centimetres.
  _____    _____

- How much further did Josh's car go than Leah's car?
  _____

- How many cars travelled more than 10cm?
  _____

Can you make up a question about the investigation?

. . . and then answer it.

- [ _____ ]

Andrew Brodie Publications © A & C Black Publishers Ltd.

Across the Curriculum: Science for ages 6–7 | FORCES AND MOVEMENT | DT | 6

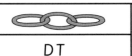

Name:    Date:

## Build a wind-powered boat

Can your group make the boat that moves fastest?

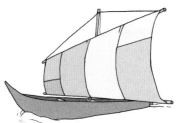

- Work in pairs or groups of three.

- You have a selection of things from which to make a boat.

- Think carefully about which items you will use.

- You want to make a boat which will move across the water faster than any of the other boats made.

- Draw a labelled diagram of your boat showing what you need to make it.

- Write about why you think you have chosen good materials to make a boat that will travel quickly.

- When you have made your boat, test it to make sure it doesn't sink or topple over.

- Now think of a way to find out which of the boats is fastest.

Enjoy doing your investigation to find the fastest boat.

Andrew Brodie Publications © A & C Black Publishers Ltd.

**7** | Across the Curriculum: Science for ages 6–7 | **FORCES AND MOVEMENT** | DT

Name:                    Date:

## 'Build a vehicle' challenge

*An activity for 2 or 3 children.*

- You have been given some construction toys.

- Choose what you think would be best to use to make a vehicle.

- Your vehicle must not have more than four wheels.

- Your vehicle must be able to carry a small roll of sticky tape.

- Your vehicle must be no longer or wider than the black line around these instructions.

- When you have finished test your vehicle to see how well it does its job.

- Draw a labelled diagram showing how your vehicle was made.

Can you make up an investigation to see which groups have made the best vehicles?

Across the Curriculum
Science for ages 6–7

# USING ELECTRICITY

Curriculum Links

We show possible curriculum links but we will not have thought of everything so you may like to add some of your own.

**Literacy**
Wide range of vocabulary related to electricity and electrical items. Writing rules for safety. Alphabetical order.

**RE**
Use of electricity in places of worship.

**DT**
Making circuit for bulb to light inside DT model.

**History**
Change in items used in homes due to the advent of electricity. Comparing the past to the present.

**Using Electricity**

**Geography**
How electricity helps global travel and communications (computers, etc).

**Numeracy**
Problem solving. Use of electrical items as stimulus for practising ten times table and five times table. Measuring in centimetres.

Andrew Brodie Publications © A & C Black Publishers Ltd.

| Across the Curriculum Science for ages 6–7 | USING ELECTRICITY | Teachers' Notes |

Worksheet 1 is designed to be used after children have made simple complete circuits and is suitable for assessment.

Worksheet 2 contains relevant vocabulary regarding electrical items.

Worksheet 3 is suitable for classroom use or homework. It is also good for pairs or small groups and can encourage the use of simple dictionaries for correct spelling. An alternative is to enlarge the sheet and use it as an ongoing class activity. This work will help the children to realise just how many everyday items are electrically powered (mains or battery). There are inevitably a few letters for which it is unlikely the children will think of an item.

Worksheet 4 is suitable for enlarging. Use the results for classroom display or for use as a class book of safety rules. It is important that children understand the dangers of electricity. Discussion prior to completing this sheet should ensure children begin their rule with either <u>always</u> or <u>never</u>. Encourage correct, bold, easy to read writing and a large clear illustration.

Worksheet 5 illustrates electrical equipment as a stimulus for counting in tens, counting in fives and measurement using centimetres.

Worksheets 6 and 7 are designed to further develop the children's understanding that people in the past existed without electricity in the home.

Across the Curriculum: Science for ages 6–7

USING ELECTRICITY

Literacy

1

Name:

Date:

## Will it work?

- Look at each picture carefully and decide whether the bulb will light.

- Under each picture answer the question and give the reason for your answer.

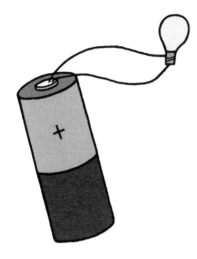

Will it work? _____ because

_____

_____

Will it work? _____ because

_____

_____

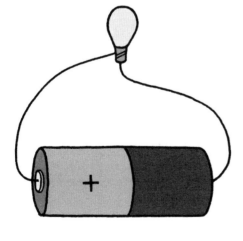

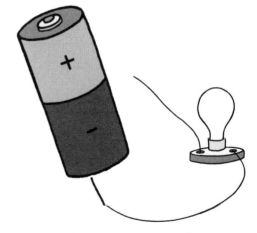

Will it work? _____ because

_____

_____

Will it work? _____ because

_____

_____

Andrew Brodie Publications © A & C Black Publishers Ltd.

| | | | | **USING ELECTRICITY** | | | | Literacy |

**2** Across the Curriculum: Science for ages 6–7

Name:   Date:

## Wordsearch

- Look at the words in the box. They are all words about electricity or items that use electricity.

- Make sure you can read every word and that you understand the meaning of each word.

- Now find the words in the wordsearch.

- They might be written horizontally →, vertically ↓ or diagonally ↘.

### WORD BANK

plug   socket   mains   connection

television   computer   circuit   electricity

wire   freezer   switch   battery

light bulb   vacuum cleaner

| p | i | b | e | l | e | c | t | r | i | c | i | t | y |
|---|---|---|---|---|---|---|---|---|---|---|---|---|---|
| l | l | e |   | z | c | g | p | k | c | e | l | s |   |
| a | k | u |   | c | i | o |   |   | o | n | p | l |   |
| m | r | z | g | n | o | r | o |   | n | c | f | i |   |
| v | a | c | u | u | m | c | l | e | a | n | e | r | g |
| l | x | i | s | a | p | u | r | r | t | e | v | e | h |
| n | e | e | n | e | u | i | l | s | o | c | k | e | t |
| o |   |   | i | s | t | t | m | k | w | t | r | z | b |
| r |   |   | a | v | e | r |   | n | i | v | e | u |   |
| b | a | t | t | e | r | y |   | s | o | r | r | l |   |
| o | l | v | s | w | i | t | c | h | p | n | r | e | b |
| t | e | l | e | v | i | s | i | o | n | z | o | x | e |

Across the Curriculum: Science for ages 6–7

**USING ELECTRICITY**

Literacy

3

Name:                              Date:

# An electrical alphabet

- For each letter of the alphabet, try to think of something that usually uses electricity. (For example, c = computer or CD player.)
- Some letters will be easy to find words for. You may not be able to think of something for a few letters.

| | | | |
|---|---|---|---|
| a | | n | |
| b | | o | |
| c | | p | |
| d | | q | |
| e | | r | |
| f | | s | |
| g | | t | |
| h | | u | |
| i | | v | |
| j | | w | |
| k | | x | |
| l | | y | |
| m | | z | |

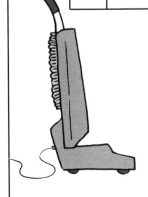  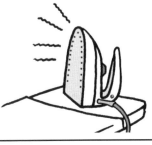 

Andrew Brodie Publications © A & C Black Publishers Ltd.

**4** | Across the Curriculum: Science for ages 6–7 | **USING ELECTRICITY** |
Literacy

Name:  Date:

### Electricity is dangerous

- Make up an important rule to help people to stay safe.
- Write your rule on the poster below.
- Draw a good picture to go with it.

---

# Electricity is Dangerous

*Follow the rule and keep safe!*

# USING ELECTRICITY

*Across the Curriculum: Science for ages 6–7*

Numeracy — 5

Name:      Date:

## Problems

1 box has 10 bulbs.

3 boxes have _____ bulbs.

5 boxes have _____ bulbs.

10 boxes have _____ bulbs.

1 pack has 5 batteries

2 packs have _____ batteries.

6 packs have _____ batteries.

7 packs have _____ batteries.

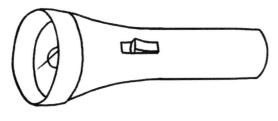

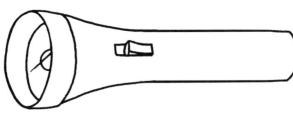

Carefully measure the length of each torch.

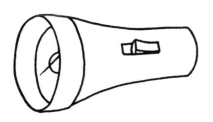

Colour the 5cm torch blue.

Colour the 10cm torch red.

Colour the 7cm torch green.

Colour the 8cm torch yellow.

# USING ELECTRICITY

Across the Curriculum Science for ages 6–7

History

Name:  Date:

## Before electricity

- The pictures on the left show items that were used in homes for many years before electricity was used. The pictures on the right show the electrical items that replaced them.
- First label each item.
- Match each old item to its modern equivalent. One has been done for you.

**WORD BANK**

electric blanket    copper kettle
light bulb    warming pan
candle    broom    electric iron
electric kettle    flat iron
vacuum cleaner

open fire

electric fire

Across the Curriculum: Science for ages 6–7

USING ELECTRICITY

History

7

Name:                                  Date:

## Out of time

- Look at this picture. It shows the inside of a house many years ago, before electricity was used.
- The artist has included things that shouldn't be on the picture, as they are all things that use electricity.
- Mark each of the misplaced items with a cross (x).

- Make a list of the items you found.

_____     _____

_____     _____

_____     _____

_____     _____

_____

- Now colour the picture.

Andrew Brodie Publications © A & C Black Publishers Ltd.

# SPARE WEB PAGE

Across the Curriculum Science for ages 6–7

Curriculum Links

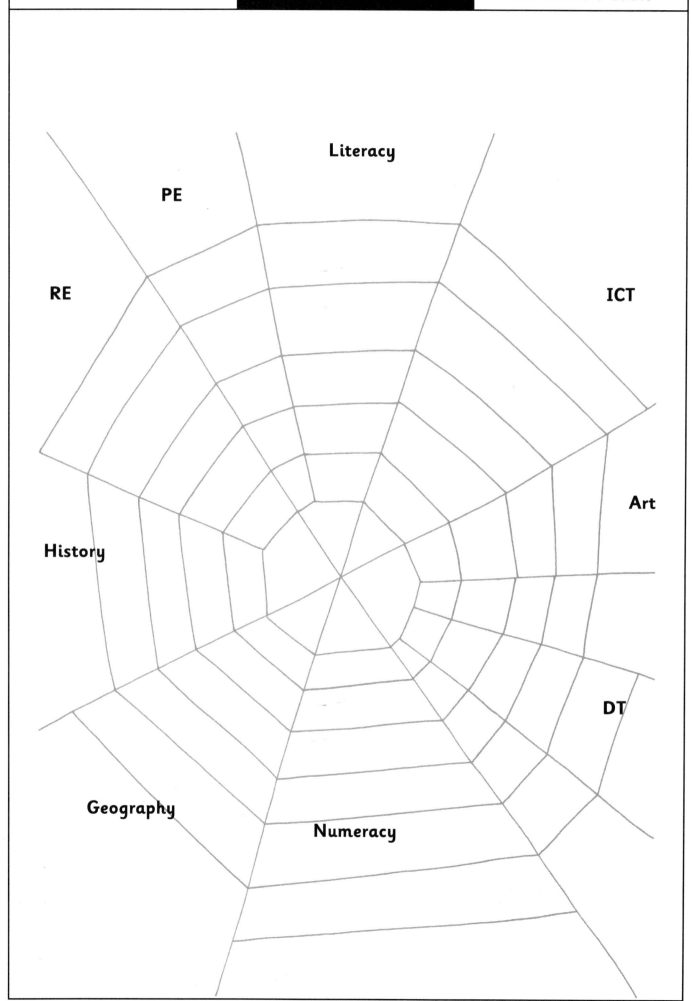